The Instinct for Cooperation:

A Graphic Novel Conversation with Noam Chomsky

Written by Jeffrey Wilson

Illustrated by Eliseu Gouveia

Lettered by Jay Jacot

Seven Stories Press

New York • Oakland • London

Seven Stories Press
140 Watts Street
New York, NY 10013
www.sevenstories.com

Library of Congress Cataloging-in-Publication Data is on file.

ISBN 978-1-60980-816-7 (pbk)
ISBN 978-1-60980-817-4 (ebook)

Printed in the USA.

9 8 7 6 5 4 3 2 1

For Rachel and all those creating spaces
for resistance and trouble making.

Contents

Chapter 1

Human Nature and Cooperation

THERE'S NOTHING PARTICULARLY UNIQUE ABOUT THIS PHOTO.
ONE OF HUNDREDS, PROBABLY THOUSANDS THAT CHOMSKY HAS TAKEN ON ENDLESS SPEAKING TOURS OVER THE DECADES WITH FANS OF HIS WRITING LIKE ME.
THIS IS NOAM CHOMSKY (NC).
YOU'LL COME TO BETTER KNOW HIS THOUGHTS AND IDEAS.
THAT'S ME, JEFF (JW).
AND MY BUDDY GABE MAKING HIS ONLY APPEARANCE IN THE COMIC.

JW: THAT EXPERIENCE OF MEETING CHOMSKY AND THE WALK HOME AFTER GOT THE "WHEELS TURNING," AS THE SAYING GOES.
UMM, MAYBE I SHOULD INTERVIEW CHOMSKY ABOUT THE OCCUPY WALL STREET MOVEMENT? IT'D BE GREAT TO USE FOR MY COURSE.
AT THE TIME I THOUGHT IT WOULD BE PERFECT TO USE FOR A UNIT ON SOCIAL MOVEMENTS THAT I WAS TEACHING AT A LOCAL COMMUNITY COLLEGE.

SO WITH A LITTLE HELP FROM GABE AND AFTER A FEW E-MAILS...

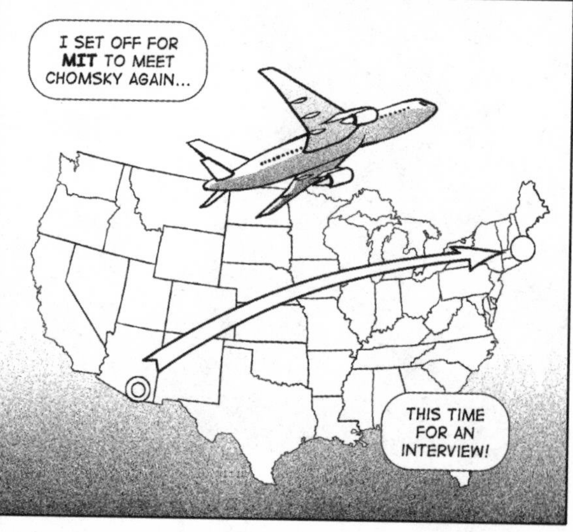
I SET OFF FOR **MIT** TO MEET CHOMSKY AGAIN...
THIS TIME FOR AN INTERVIEW!

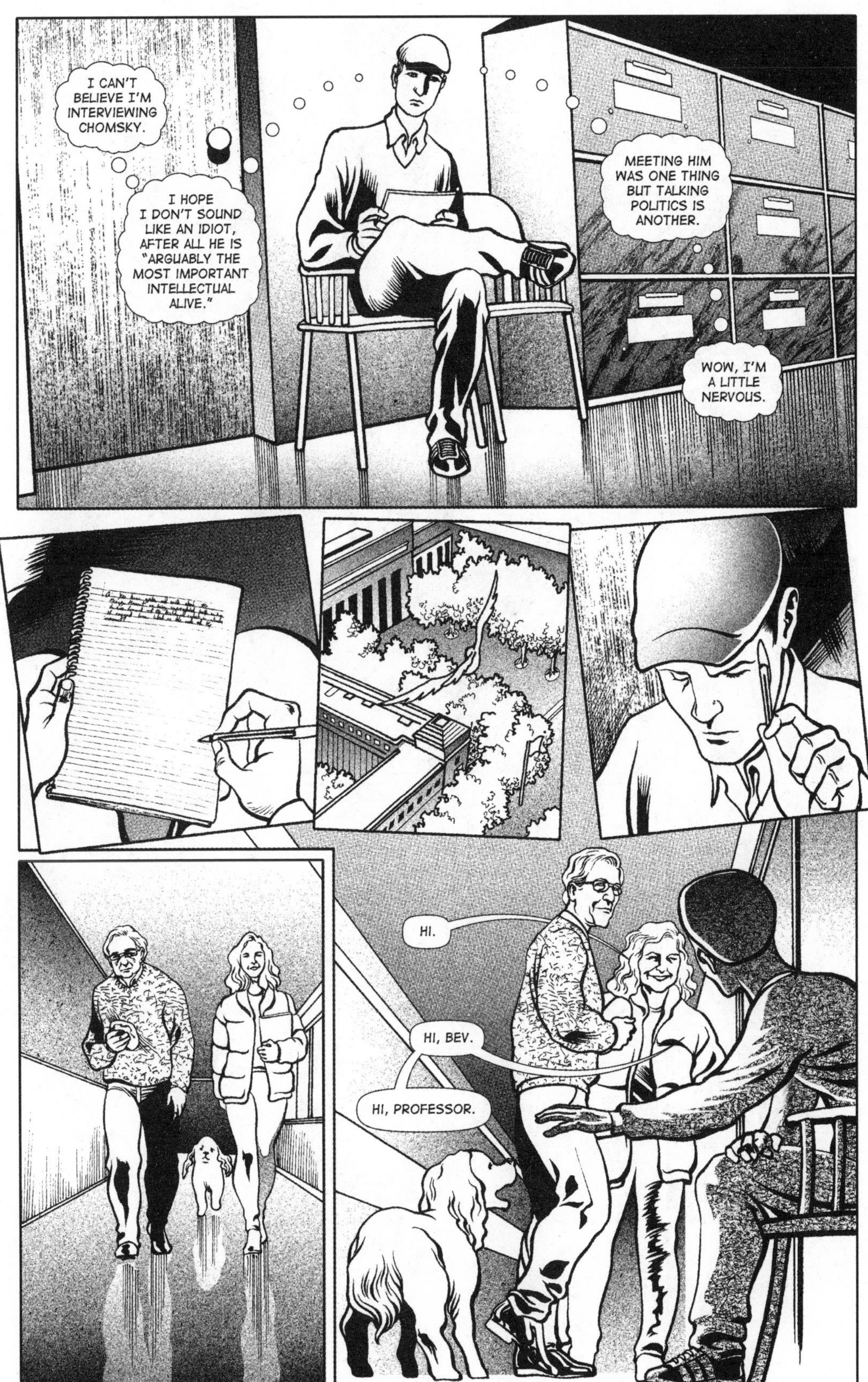
I CAN'T BELIEVE I'M INTERVIEWING CHOMSKY.
I HOPE I DON'T SOUND LIKE AN IDIOT, AFTER ALL HE IS "ARGUABLY THE MOST IMPORTANT INTELLECTUAL ALIVE."
MEETING HIM WAS ONE THING BUT TALKING POLITICS IS ANOTHER.
WOW, I'M A LITTLE NERVOUS.
HI.
HI, BEV.
HI, PROFESSOR.

YEAH, JEFF, HE'S FINISHING UP LUNCH.
WOULD YOU LIKE TO WAIT IN HIS OFFICE?
FEEL FREE TO LOOK AROUND.
THANK YOU.
CHOMSKY'S LONGTIME ASSISTANT BEV LET ME INTO THE OFFICE.
THANKS FOR TAKING THE TIME TO MEET WITH ME.

HI, JEFF, HAVE A SEAT.
TELL ME A LITTLE BIT ABOUT YOURSELF.
NOT SURE IF YOU REMEMBER BUT WE MET IN TUCSON ABOUT A YEAR AGO.
I TEACH AT A COMMUNITY COLLEGE.
I'M TOYING WITH THE IDEA OF MOVING TO ARIZONA FOR THE WINTERS.
REALLY?
WELL, WINTERS ARE GREAT, BUT SUMMERS ARE BRUTAL.
STILL HAVEN'T DECIDED YET.
WHAT DID YOU WANT TO TALK WITH ME ABOUT?

three passions, simple but overwhelmingly strong, have governed my life: the longing for love, the search for knowledge, and unbearable pity for the suffering of mankind BERTRAND RUSSELL
Membership Card
I WOULD LIKE TO START BY DISCUSSING THE "OCCUPY WALL STREET" MOVEMENT...
REC
N CUT
EASY
23:32:14

three passions, simple but overwhelmingly strong have governed my life: the longing for love, the search for knowledge, and unbearable pity for the suffering of mankind
BERTRAND RUSSELL
I'M INTERESTED IN THE "DEEPER STRUCTURE" OF THE MOVEMENT,
SPECIFICALLY THE SMALLER SOCIAL SYSTEMS OPERATING IN IT,
THE KITCHEN, LIBRARY, HEALTH SERVICES, AS FORMS OF MUTUAL AID.
YOU'VE DISCUSSED THIS IN OTHER INTERVIEWS,
BUT I'D LIKE TO GO INTO A LITTLE MORE DEPTH.
WHAT DO YOU VIEW AS THE HISTORICAL CONTEXT OF THESE SPECIFIC ASPECTS OF OCCUPY?

THEY JUST CAME SPONTANEOUSLY. NOBODY PLANNED THEM.
WHEN PEOPLE FOUND THEMSELVES TOGETHER IN A SPACE, THEIR NATURAL INSTINCTS CAME OUT.

UMMM, NATURAL INSTINCTS?
I WAS EXPECTING A CONVERSATION ABOUT HISTORY AND POLITICS.
COULD YOU ELABORATE?

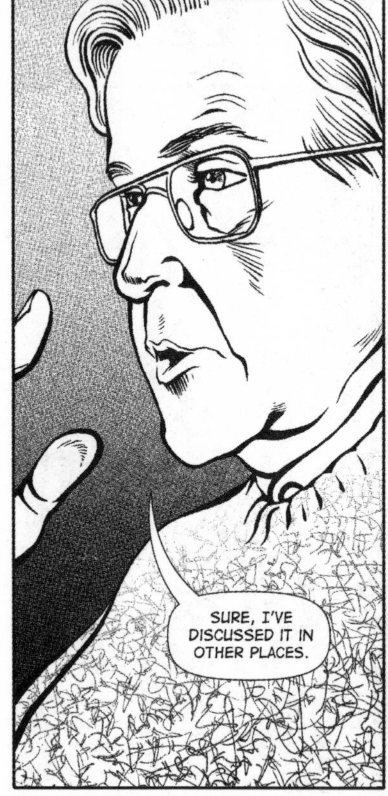

NC: MY VIEW IS "FUNDAMENTAL HUMAN NEEDS" PROBABLY INVOLVE "SPONTANEOUS INITIATIVE, CREATIVE WORK, SOLIDARITY, AND PURSUIT OF SOCIAL JUSTICE."
THE SCHOLAR WILHELM VON HUMBOLDT MADE A SIMILAR POINT, WHICH I'VE WRITTEN ABOUT...

"TO INQUIRE AND TO CREATE."
"THESE ARE THE CENTRES AROUND WHICH ALL HUMAN PURSUITS MORE OR LESS DIRECTLY REVOLVE."
WILHELM VON HUMBOLDT: GERMAN PHILOSOPHER AND FOUNDER OF THE HUMBOLDT UNIVERSITY OF BERLIN

MIKHAIL BAKUNIN WROTE OF AN "INSTINCT FOR FREEDOM."
MIKHAIL BAKUNIN: RUSSIAN REVOLUTIONARY ANARCHIST

IF WE ARE TO MOVE TOWARD A DECENT SOCIETY...

OR HAVE SOME VISION OF A FUTURE SOCIETY,
THESE ASPECTS OF HUMAN NATURE OUTLINED BY VON HUMBOLDT AND BAKUNIN WILL NEED TO BE ACCOMMODATED.

IF I UNDERSTAND YOU CORRECTLY,
THERE IS A CONNECTION BETWEEN HUMAN NATURE AND CREATIVITY?
BUT HOW DOES THIS RELATE TO OCCUPY?
RIGHT,
"NOW MY OWN FEELING IS THAT THE FUNDAMENTAL HUMAN CAPACITY,"
LIKE I'VE SAID OTHER PLACES,
"THE CAPACITY AND THE NEED FOR CREATIVE SELF-EXPRESSION, FOR FREE CONTROL OF ALL ASPECTS OF ONE'S LIFE AND THOUGHT."
SO WHEN YOU ASKED ME ABOUT THE HISTORICAL CONTEXT OF OCCUPY, IT STARTS WITH PEOPLE'S NATURAL INSTINCTS.
AND YOUR NATURAL INSTINCTS ARE COOPERATION, MUTUAL SUPPORT, BONDS OF ASSOCIATION, HELPING ONE ANOTHER.

OCCUPY WALL STREET
BASIC FIRST AID
NC: YOU'RE GOING TO NEED HEALTH SERVICES.
FINE, WE'LL SET UP A HEALTH SERVICE AND PEOPLE WILL RUN IT.
WE WANT TO READ THINGS, WE'LL GET PEOPLE TO DONATE BOOKS AND HAVE A LIBRARY.
LIBRARY
INCIDENTALLY THE POWER STRUCTURES WERE VERY WORRIED ABOUT THE LIBRARY.

NC: YOU MAY HAVE NOTICED THAT WHEN THE POLICE CAME IN UNDER BLOOMBERG'S ORDERS AND SMASHED UP ZUCCOTTI PARK [LOCATION OF OCCUPY WALL STREET]...
ONE OF THE THINGS THEY DID WAS DESTROY ALL THE BOOKS.
YOU HAVE GOT TO DESTROY BOOKS THAT ARE DANGEROUS.
IT HAS A LONG TRADITION BACK TO THE MIDDLE AGES.
ARIZONA KNOWS ALL ABOUT THAT.

Chapter 2

Tucson Knows All About That!

YEAH, WE KNOW ALL ABOUT THAT.
IN APRIL OF 2010 ARIZONA PASSED HOUSE BILL 2281.
IT TARGETED THE HIGHLY SUCCESSFUL MEXICAN AMERICAN STUDIES PROGRAM AT TUCSON HIGH SCHOOL.
CONCEIVED BY CONSERVATIVE POLITICIAN TOM HORNE AND IMPLEMENTED BY JOHN HUPPENTHAL, THE BILL PROHIBITS CLASSES THAT:
1. PROMOTE THE OVERTHROW OF THE UNITED STATES GOVERNMENT.
2. PROMOTE RESENTMENT TOWARD A RACE OR CLASS OF PEOPLE.
3. ARE DESIGNED PRIMARILY FOR PUPILS OF A PARTICULAR ETHNIC GROUP.
4. ADVOCATE ETHNIC SOLIDARITY INSTEAD OF THE TREATMENT OF PUPILS AS INDIVIDUALS.
TOM HORNE, SUPERINTENDENT OF PUBLIC INSTRUCTION, 2003–2011
JOHN HUPPENTHAL, SUPERINTENDENT OF PUBLIC INSTRUCTION, 2011–2015
EDUCATION
TUCSON UNIFIED SCHO
JW: THE MEXICAN AMERICAN STUDIES (MAS) PROGRAM IN TUCSON WAS FOUND TO BE ILLEGAL UNDER THE NEW LAW AND WAS DISMANTLED AFTER THE PASSING OF HB 2281.
SAVE OUR RIGHT TO AN EDUCATION
SO THAT'S WHAT CHOMSKY WAS REFERENCING.
WHAT FOLLOWS ARE INTERVIEWS WITH INDIVIDUALS INVOLVED IN MAS.

CURTIS ACOSTA (CA): FORMER MEXICAN AMERICAN STUDIES TEACHER AT TUCSON HIGH SCHOOL.
PRESSURE TO GET RID OF THE PROGRAM GOES BACK FURTHER THAN HB 2281,
BUT THE TROUBLE REALLY STARTED WITH THE DOLORES HUERTA SPEECH AND THAT ONE LINE.

REPUBLICANS HATE LATINOS.
DOLORES HUERTA, GUEST SPEAKER, TUCSON HIGH SCHOOL 2006

CA: IT WASN'T A LONG SPEECH. IT'S TOO BAD IT GOT REDUCED TO THAT LINE.
SHE HAD A Q/A AFTERWARDS AND ONE OF MY STUDENTS IN THE AUDITORIUM WAS CONSERVATIVE. I TOLD HIM...

GET UP THERE MIJO.
GO ASK HER A QUESTION.
HE DIDN'T GET A CHANCE TO ASK,
BUT THAT SPEECH MADE HORNE CONSCIOUS OF OUR PROGRAM.
HE SAID, "IT'S NOT LIKE WE SHOULDN'T HAVE CONTROVERSIAL SPEAKERS, BUT THEY NEED TO HEAR THE OTHER SIDE."
WITH DOLORES THE "LEFT" AND HIM THE "RIGHT," WHICH IS A BINARY I REJECT.
THERE ARE MORE THAN TWO SIDES TO EVERYTHING. IT'S MORE COMPLEX THAN THAT.

CA: ANYWAY, HORNE WAS ALREADY AGAINST MAS.
I BELIEVE HE SAID SOMETHING LIKE, "I WILL SEE THE END OF THE MEXICAN AMERICAN STUDIES PROGRAM" BEFORE HE EVEN SPOKE AT THE HIGH SCHOOL.
JUST TO GIVE YOU AN IDEA OF HIS POLITICS, HE HAD ALREADY RUN ON AN ANTI-BILINGUAL, ANTI-WOMEN'S STUDY PLATFORM.
HIS FIRST ELECTION FLYER LISTED HIS ACCOMPLISHMENTS AS ENDING WOMEN'S STUDIES IN PARADISE VALLEY [A TOWN IN ARIZONA] AS A SCHOOL BOARD MEMBER.
THIS DUDE WAS REALLY CLEAR ABOUT DESTROYING THE TYPE OF EDUCATIONAL EQUITY AND EQUALITY OUR PRINCIPLES EXPOUND.
BUT LIKE I WAS SAYING HE WAS COMING DOWN TO REPRESENT THE "OTHER SIDE" AND THE STUDENTS WERE GIVEN A LAUNDRY LIST OF NO'S! BEFORE THE SPEECH.
NO QUESTION AND ANSWER!
NO SIGNAGE!
NO BACKPACKS!
THEY WERE SUPPOSED TO COME IN AND GET THE STUMP SPEECH AND BE PASSIVE RECEPTACLES.

OK, SO GET THIS FOR PATRIARCHY.
HORNE DOESN'T SPEAK.
HE BRINGS HIS DEPUTY SUPERINTENDENT OF INSTRUCTION BECAUSE SHE IS LATINA, SHE'S CHICANA AND SHE SPEAKS.
HE SITS BEHIND HER ON THE ONLY CHAIR ON STAGE!
THE YOUNG ONES WEREN'T GOING TO TAKE THIS.
OU CAN
SI

THEY HAD AN ACTION.

IT WAS PRETTY REMARKABLE.

I MEAN HOW DISRESPECTFUL, THE OFFICE OF THE STATE SUPERINTENDENT OF PUBLIC INSTRUCTION COMES TO ADDRESS HIS STUDENTS...
AND THEY DON'T WANT TO HAVE A QUESTION AND ANSWER.
ARE YOU KIDDING ME? THE YOUNG ONES WERE NOT GOING TO LET THAT HAPPEN,
AND THEY DIDN'T.
THANKS.
SO I WAS SAYING?
OH RIGHT,
HORNE LOVES PASSIVE, DOMESTICATED, DOCILE STUDENTS AND WHAT HE GOT WAS AN ACTION.
THAT WAS THE STRAW THAT STIRRED THE DRINK AND IT WAS ON.
AFTER THAT HE WAS TOTALLY COMMITTED TO ENDING THE PROGRAM.

RENE M. (RM): FORMER MEXICAN AMERICAN STUDIES TEACHER
HI, JEFF.
RENE, THANKS SO MUCH FOR MEETING ME.

WHAT HAPPENED AFTER HORNE'S ASSISTANT SPOKE AT TUCSON HIGH SCHOOL?
WELL, HB 2281 IS EVENTUALLY PASSED AND JOHN HUPPENTHAL BECOMES THE NEW SUPERINTENDENT OF INSTRUCTION.

WITH THE LAW PASSED HE THEN NEEDS TO FIND MAS IN VIOLATION OF THE LAW TO GET TOTALLY RID OF IT.

SO IN ORDER TO DO THIS HE PICKS AND HIRES A FIRM TO AUDIT THE PROGRAM TO BASICALLY FIND US IN VIOLATION OF THE LAW.
IT'S CRAZY, THE AUDIT COSTS OVER $100,000.
WOW, THAT'S EXPENSIVE.
SO WHAT WAS IT LIKE HAVING THE AUDITORS COMING INTO THE CLASSROOM?

RM: IT WAS EXHAUSTING JUST BEING EVALUATED CONTINUALLY...

WHETHER IT'S BY A SITE ADMINISTRATOR...

OR A DISTRICT ADMINISTRATOR,
OR THE AUDITORS.

WE WERE CONSTANTLY UNDER SURVEILLANCE.

RM: IT WAS INTERESTING DURING THAT TIME TOO 'CAUSE THE STUDENTS WERE MUCH MORE QUIET. THEY WERE UNEASY. THEY WEREN'T THEMSELVES.
THE AUDITORS LOOKED AT EVERYTHING DOWN TO THE POSTERS ON THE WALL;
THEY WERE TAKING NOTES ON EVERY POWERPOINT SLIDE.
I MEAN EVERYTHING.
WE THOUGHT THERE WAS NO WAY THAT THE AUDIT COULD COME OUT FAVORABLY FOR US.
I MEAN REALLY WE THOUGHT THE PROGRAM WAS OVER. BUT IT ENDS UP BLOWING UP IN HUPPENTHAL'S FACE.
THE AUDIT SAYS, WE DON'T VIOLATE THE LAW, WE ARE DOING GREAT THINGS AND IN FACT THIS PROGRAM NEEDS TO BE EXPANDED.
WHAT'S HE GOING TO DO?
RM: HE HAS A PRESS CONFERENCE DECLARING THAT...
THE PROGRAM VIOLATES THE LAW DESPITE THE FINDINGS OF HIS AUDIT,
THE ONE HE HIRED.
NOW THE EXTERNAL AUDIT FAILED TO PROVIDE A COMPREHENSIVE REVIEW.
EVEN IN THE FACE OF THIS HYPOCRISY, MAS WAS STILL DEEMED ILLEGAL AND DISMANTLED.

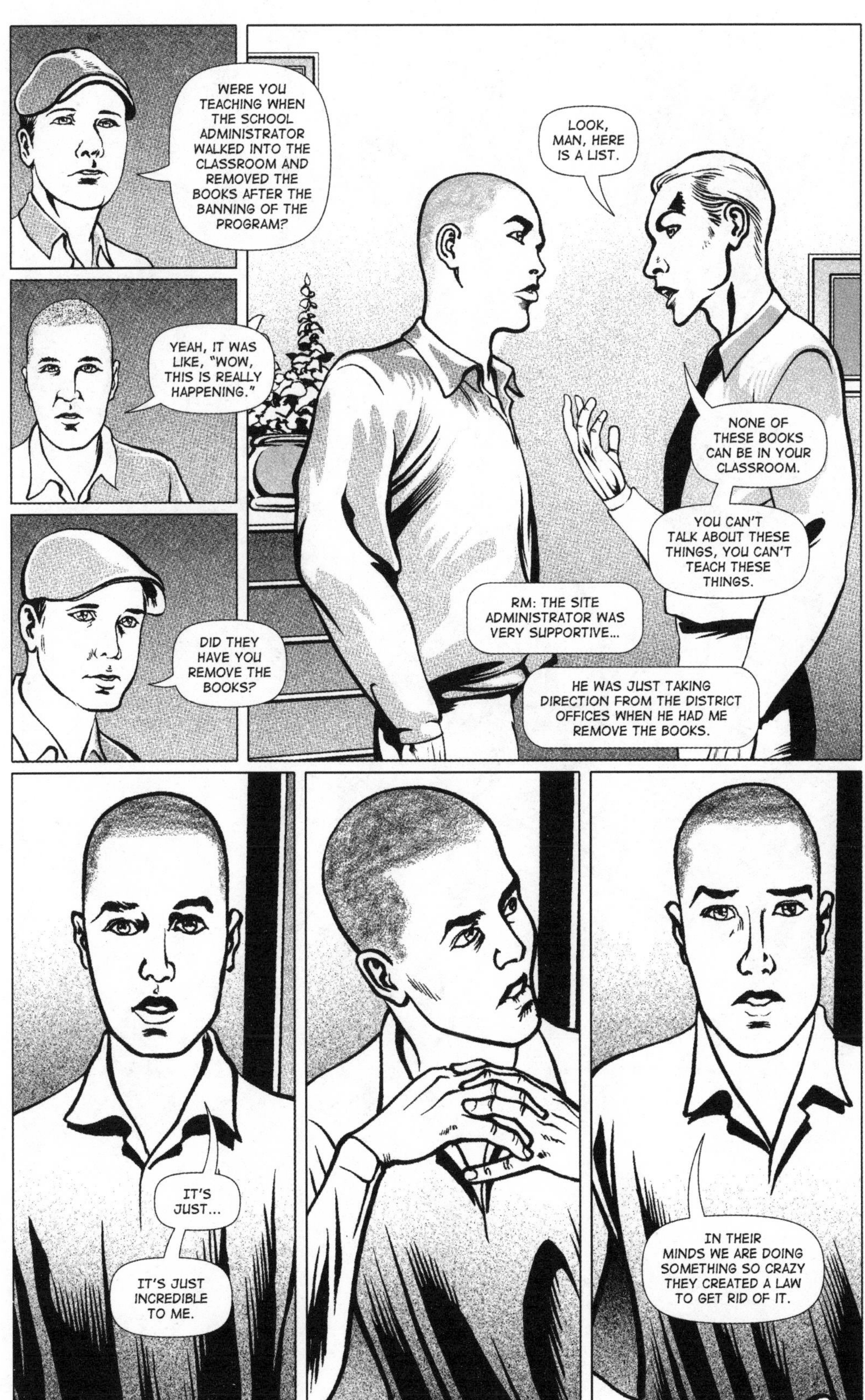
WERE YOU TEACHING WHEN THE SCHOOL ADMINISTRATOR WALKED INTO THE CLASSROOM AND REMOVED THE BOOKS AFTER THE BANNING OF THE PROGRAM?
LOOK, MAN, HERE IS A LIST.
YEAH, IT WAS LIKE, "WOW, THIS IS REALLY HAPPENING."
NONE OF THESE BOOKS CAN BE IN YOUR CLASSROOM.
YOU CAN'T TALK ABOUT THESE THINGS, YOU CAN'T TEACH THESE THINGS.
DID THEY HAVE YOU REMOVE THE BOOKS?
RM: THE SITE ADMINISTRATOR WAS VERY SUPPORTIVE...
HE WAS JUST TAKING DIRECTION FROM THE DISTRICT OFFICES WHEN HE HAD ME REMOVE THE BOOKS.
IT'S JUST...
IT'S JUST INCREDIBLE TO ME.
IN THEIR MINDS WE ARE DOING SOMETHING SO CRAZY THEY CREATED A LAW TO GET RID OF IT.

Save Ethnic Studies
Quetzalcoatl
Quetzalcoatl
Quetzalcoatl
Quetzalcoatl
WE ARE AMERICA
ARABIC ALPHABET
My Revolution is born out of love for My People. Not HATRED For Others.
RM: THEY SAID THE BOOKS WEREN'T BANNED, JUST "BOXED AND STORED" AS PART OF THE DISMANTLING OF MAS.
BUT THE RESULT IS THE SAME.

CURTIS, I SPOKE WITH RENÉ ABOUT HAVING TO REMOVE BOOKS LIKE *THE TEMPEST*, *PEDAGOGY OF THE OPPRESSED* AND *RETHINKING COLUMBUS* FROM THIS CLASSROOM.
COULD YOU TAKE ME INTO THE CLASSROOM?
WHAT WAS IT LIKE TEACHING MAS AT TUCSON HIGH SCHOOL?
WHAT MADE THE PROGRAM SO SPECIAL?
IT WAS THE GREATEST PLACE I'VE EVER BEEN.
"Por Mi Raza, Habla El Espíritu" Movimiento Estudian Chicano de Aztlan
AND NOT BECAUSE IT WAS MY CLASSROOM, IT WAS *OUR* CLASSROOM.
I'LL NEVER BE THAT HAPPY AGAIN.
I MEAN I HAVE TWO SONS THAT I LOVE AND A WIFE I CAN'T GET ENOUGH OF AND A FAMILY...
SO OF COURSE I'M *PLENTY* HAPPY.
BUT THERE WAS THIS PARTICULAR TYPE OF HAPPINESS IN THE CLASSROOM.

CA: IT WAS A LIBERATED, TRULY HUMANIZED CLASSROOM...
AN EDUCATIONAL KIND OF HAPPY THAT I PROBABLY WON'T EVER REPLICATE.
IF PEOPLE WANT TO KNOW THE SECRET... IT WAS ALL LOVE.
IT WAS A FORMALIZED...
THEORETICALLY INTENTIONAL...
EDUCATIONAL STANCE TO INSERT LOVE AT THE CENTER OF EVERYTHING.
IT WAS RADICAL LOVE.

ALANNA C. (AC): FORMER MAS STUDENT
AC: HOW WOULD I BE DIFFERENT IF I DIDN'T TAKE MAS CLASSES?
I'LL GIVE YOU WHERE I WAS, AS OPPOSED TO WHERE I AM NOW.
SO, BEFORE [THE PROGRAM] MY IDEA WAS...
DAILY SPECIALS
ICED COFFEE $2
FRENCH SODA $3
I'M GONNA FINISH HIGH SCHOOL. I WAS GONNA GO TO COSMETOLOGY SCHOOL TO BE A NAIL TECH AND PUT MYSELF THROUGH COLLEGE.
I FIGURED BY THE TIME I WAS 21 I SHOULD'VE BEEN...
INTERNATIONAL CLIPPERS
GRADUATED AND PREGNANT UNDER MY CAP AND GOWN...
AND MARRIED.
THAT'S WHAT I WAS GOING TO DO BEFORE.

WHERE DO YOU THINK THOSE IDEAS OF GETTING MARRIED AND HAVING CHILDREN AT A YOUNGER AGE CAME FROM?
IT'S THAT CYCLICAL THING.
MY PARENTS WERE MARRIED AT 20 OR 21 AND NEITHER OF THEM WENT TO COLLEGE.

SO MY PARENTS WERE LIKE, "YOU'RE GOING TO COLLEGE."
OKAY, WELL, I'LL GO TO COLLEGE. BUT WHAT AM I GONNA DO? I'LL BE AN ULTRASOUND TECHNICIAN, THAT'S COOL.

OR I'M GONNA DO NAILS FOR A LIVING.
THOSE ARE NOT BAD CAREERS AND YOU CAN HAVE GREAT CLIENTELE OR WORK IN A LOT OF DIFFERENT CLINICS OR HOSPITALS. THAT'S GREAT.
BUT THE PROGRAM WAS THE FIRST TIME THAT IT WAS SUGGESTED THAT I COULD DO SOMETHING DIFFERENT.
THAT I'M NOT LIVING UP TO MY POTENTIAL.
NOW MY GOALS ARE MUCH DIFFERENT. I'M STILL 2 1/2 YEARS AWAY FROM GRADUATING COLLEGE.
I WANT TO BE A SCREENWRITER. I'M NOT MARRIED, I DON'T HAVE ANY KIDS AND THE THING I'M LOOKING MOST FORWARD TO IS TRAVELING THE WORLD, YOU KNOW, SEEING WHAT'S OUT THERE.

I DIDN'T HAVE THOSE INTENTIONS BEFORE.
I MEAN WHO'S TO SAY IF I HADN'T TAKEN MEXICAN AMERICAN STUDIES MY VIEWS WOULD'VE CHANGED, BUT FOR ME THOSE VIEWS CHANGED RIGHT AWAY.

IT MADE ME MORE CURIOUS TO SEE WHAT ELSE WAS OUT THERE, TO SEE THE WORLD BEYOND MY FOUR WALLS.

WHAT'S THE MOST IMPORTANT THING YOU LEARNED FROM BEING IN THE PROGRAM?
IT'S LEARNING TO BE HUMBLE.
IT'S ABOUT REMINDING MYSELF THAT I'M NO DIFFERENT FROM THESE LADIES.
I'M NO BETTER, I'M NO WORSE.

LEARNING TO BE HAPPY WITH THE THINGS YOU KNOW AND NOT THE THINGS YOU HAVE.
REALLY, IT'S LEARNING TO BE MORE HUMAN.

Chapter 3

Democracy and Sproul Plaza

PROFESSOR, COULD WE RETURN TO THE OCCUPY MOVEMENT?
YOU MENTIONED EARLIER THAT THE MOVEMENT WAS SPONTANEOUS, COULD YOU TALK A LITTLE MORE ABOUT THAT?
SURE, I THINK IT'S A REFLECTION OF THE SPONTANEOUS CHARACTER OF PEOPLE, WHICH IS JUST DEADENED IN THIS SOCIETY.
NC: IT'S LIKE YOUR ONLINE COURSES.
ONE OF THE GOALS I THINK, I CAN'T PROVE IT, OF SHIFTING TO ONLINE COURSES IS THAT IT SEPARATES PEOPLE FROM ONE ANOTHER.
GEOG 500 SP14 001
FEB 17: 2nd Draft Research Question
AND IN FACT MANY THINGS IN THIS SOCIETY ARE DESIGNED QUITE CONSCIOUSLY TO ATOMIZE SOCIETY.

SO, IF THE IDEAL SOCIAL UNIT IS YOU AND YOUR T.V. SET
OR COMPUTER
OR SOMETHING.
NC: THEN PEOPLE ARE CONTROLLED.
PEOPLE CAN ONLY DO ANYTHING IF THEY INTERACT, IF THEY JOIN TOGETHER, IF THEY LEARN ABOUT COOPERATION.
THEN THEY CAN SEE THAT YOU CAN HAVE A DIFFERENT WORLD.
THE PEOPLE'S LIBRARY
Our Library! Please Share
SO IT IS IMPORTANT TO BLOCK IT.
AND IT'S DONE IN ALL KINDS OF WAYS.

FOR EXAMPLE, RIGHT AFTER THE '60s THERE WAS A LOT OF CONCERN ABOUT STUDENT ACTIVISM.
IN FACT, AT THE LIBERAL END OF THE SPECTRUM [REPRESENTED IN THE TRILATERAL COMMISSION REPORT CO-AUTHORED BY SAMUEL HUNTINGTON] THEY WERE CONCERNED ABOUT WHAT THEY CALLED THE...
"FAILURE OF THE INSTITUTIONS RESPONSIBLE...
SAMUEL HUNTINGTON
FOR THE INDOCTRINATION OF THE YOUNG."
STRAIGHT OUT.
COLUMBIA UNIVERSITY 1968
SNCC SIT-INS AT LUNCH COUNTERS IN THE '60s
THE THINKING WAS WE HAVE GOT TO INDOCTRINATE THE YOUTH BETTER BECAUSE LOOK...
THEY'RE GETTING INDEPENDENT,
THEY'RE THINKING FOR THEMSELVES,
THEY'RE DOING THINGS,
THEY'RE CHALLENGING AUTHORITY.

WE CAN'T HAVE THAT.

THEY SAW AN "EXCESS OF DEMOCRACY,"

PERIODIC TABLE OF THE ELEMENTS

I'VE DISCUSSED THIS IN OTHER PLACES.
"THE REPORT GIVES A VERY REVEALING INDICATION OF THE ATTITUDE OF LIBERAL WESTERN ELITES TO 'DEMOCRACY'-
NAMELY, THAT...
'DEMOCRACY' IS THREATENED WHEN SUBSTANTIAL PARTS OF THE POPULATION ACTUALLY INVOLVE THEMSELVES IN DEFENDING THEIR RIGHTS WITHIN THE POLITICAL ARENA...
AND THAT 'DEMOCRACY' CAN SURVIVE ONLY IF THEY ARE REDUCED TO APATHY AND PASSIVITY...
SO THAT THE NATURAL LEADERS CAN RULE WITHOUT IMPEDIMENT."
THIS CONCEPTION OF DEMOCRACY GOES WAY BACK.

"GOVERNMENT IS 'TO PROTECT THE MINORITY OF THE OPULENT AGAINST THE MAJORITY.'
JAMES MADISON
THAT HAS BEEN THE GUIDING PRINCIPLE OF THE DEMOCRATIC SYSTEM FROM ITS ORIGINS UNTIL TODAY.
MADISON WAS CONCERNED BY THE 'SYMPTOMS OF A LEVELING SPIRIT'
THAT HAD ALREADY APPEARED, AND WARNED 'OF THE FUTURE DANGER' IF THE RIGHT TO VOTE WOULD PLACE
'POWER OVER PROPERTY IN THE HANDS WITHOUT A SHARE IN IT.'
THOSE 'WITHOUT PROPERTY, OR THE HOPE OF ACQUIRING IT,
CANNOT BE EXPECTED TO SYMPATHIZE SUFFICIENTLY WITH ITS RIGHTS,' MADISON EXPLAINED.
HIS SOLUTION WAS TO KEEP POLITICAL POWER IN THE HANDS OF THOSE WHO,
'COME FROM AND REPRESENT THE WEALTH OF THE NATION,' THE 'MORE CAPABLE SET OF MEN,'
WITH THE GENERAL PUBLIC FRAGMENTED AND DISORGANIZED."

A WHOLE ASSAULT AGAINST THE SYSTEM OF EDUCATION TOOK OFF IN THE EARLY '70s IN REACTION TO THIS CONCERN [ABOUT DEMOCRACY].
I MEAN ON THE RIGHT IT'S MORE EXTREME, BUT IT IS SORT OF THE LIBERAL END THAT IS MORE INTERESTING, AS USUAL.
A LOT OF THINGS HAPPENED.
ONE OF THEM IS THAT UNIVERSITY ARCHITECTURE CHANGED.
SO UNIVERSITIES, THIS IS WORLDWIDE INCIDENTALLY,
UNIVERSITIES THAT WERE BUILT AFTER THE EARLY '70s ARE DESIGNED SO THAT THEY DON'T HAVE MEETING PLACES FOR STUDENTS.
NC: THERE ARE CORRIDORS TO GET FROM HERE TO THERE SO YOU DON'T HAVE THE DANGER OF PEOPLE GETTING TOGETHER.
SO THERE IS NO SPROUL PLAZA...

JW: YOU MEAN THE DEMONSTRATIONS FOR FREE SPEECH ON THE CAMPUS OF BERKELEY IN THE '60s, RIGHT?
THESE WERE LARGELY SPONTANEOUS AND TOOK PLACE IN THE PLAZA.
CORE
SIT DOWN!!

JW: THE CAMPUS RESTRICTED POLITICAL TABLING.

THERE WAS A MASSIVE DEMONSTRATION IN THE PLAZA THAT LASTED FOR DAYS.

RIGHT, MARIO SAVIO GAVE HIS FAMOUS GEARS SPEECH IN SPROUL PLAZA.

MARIO SAVIO (MS)

THERE'S A TIME WHEN THE OPERATION OF THE MACHINE BECOMES SO ODIOUS,

MAKES YOU SO SICK AT HEART, THAT YOU CAN'T TAKE PART; YOU CAN'T EVEN PASSIVELY TAKE PART.

AND YOU'VE GOT TO PUT YOUR BODIES UPON THE GEARS AND UPON THE WHEELS, UPON THE LEVERS, UPON ALL THE APPARATUS, AND YOU'VE GOT TO MAKE IT STOP.

AND YOU'VE GOT TO INDICATE TO THE PEOPLE WHO RUN IT, TO THE PEOPLE WHO OWN IT, THAT

UNLESS YOU'RE FREE, THE MACHINE WILL BE PREVENTED FROM WORKING AT ALL!

IMPORTANTLY, MANY, INCLUDING MARIO AND OTHERS INVOLVED WITH THE FREE SPEECH MOVEMENT, HAD EXPERIENCE WITH THE CIVIL RIGHTS MOVEMENT.

United States
VOTING APPLICATION
MS: MY TOUCH WITH REALITY WAS ONE PARTICULAR MOMENT DURING FREEDOM SUMMER IN MISSISSIPPI WHEN I BROUGHT SOMEBODY TO REGISTER TO VOTE.

WHAT DO
YOU WANT,
BOY?
WANNA
REDDISH.

BOY,
WHAT DO
YOU WANT?

WANNA
REDISH.

REDDISH,
WHAT'S THAT,
BOY?

MS: WE'RE NOT ALLOWED TO SAY A WORD- GOING TO WATCH THAT'S ALL.
THEY ALL SAID, "REDDISH."
WANNA REDDISH, MA'AM.
THE WORD *REGISTER* BECOMES A TWO-SYLLABLE WORD IN MISSISSIPPI AND THAT'S WHAT THEY SAID.

AND THAT WAS MY MOMENT OF REALITY, AND YOU DON'T NEED THAT MANY.

I ONLY NEEDED THAT ONE.

I DIDN'T REALIZE HOW IMPORTANT THE CIVIL RIGHTS MOVEMENT WAS IN THE DEVELOPMENT OF STUDENT ACTIVISM IN THE '60s.
IT WAS A MAJOR INFLUENCE.
AS WITH SPROUL PLAZA, ONE OF THE REASONS FOR BOTH THE SUCCESS OF THE OCCUPY MOVEMENT AND THE REPRESSION,
NC: WHICH CAME PRETTY QUICKLY, WAS A RECOGNITION THAT...
STRIKE FOR FREE SPEECH
PUBLIC SPACES MEAN PUBLIC INTERCHANGE.

Chapter 4

The People's Library

(INAUDIBLE)...
PILES OF BOOKS...
(INAUDIBLE)...
OCTOBER...
BINDINGS...
(INAUDIBLE)...
SORRY,...
SORRY,
ZACHARY...
UMM,
I CAN'T
HEAR YOU.
COULD WE
TRY TALKING
OVER SKYPE?
(INAUDIBLE)...SURE
ZACHARY L.
LIBRARIAN AT OCCUPY
WALL STREET
JW: GREAT!
THAT IS SO
MUCH BETTER.
NYC
NOW, WHERE
DID WE LEAVE
OFF?
FIRST FEW
TIMES YOU WENT
TO OCCUPY.
RIGHT, I
WENT DOWN
THERE AROUND
THE START OF
OCTOBER...

ZL: LIKE I SAID, I HAD BEEN GOING TO SEE WHAT WAS GOING ON...
USUALLY I WOULD JUST GO AND DO A LITTLE BIT OF THIS
A LITTLE BIT OF THAT.
THEY WOULD SAY, "WE NEED SOMEBODY TO DO X" AND I WOULD, YOU KNOW, VOLUNTEER.

THEN ONE DAY I NOTICED ALL OF THESE CRATES OF BOOKS...
LIKE IN PLASTIC BINS.

ALL OF THE BOOKS WERE IN THERE SO THAT THE PAGE SIDE WAS FACING OUT INSTEAD OF THE BINDING.
AND IT JUST... IT BOTHERED ME...
SO I STARTED FLIPPING ALL THE BOOKS AROUND.

HI!
THANKS FOR HELPING OUT.
I'M PART OF THE LIBRARY WORKING GROUP.
OH, WELL, CAN I JOIN THE WORKING GROUP?

AFTER THAT EVERY SPARE MOMENT I HAD WAS DOWN THERE DOING LIBRARY STUFF.
AND MANY OF MY NOT SPARE MOMENTS.
SO AFTER YOU GOT INVOLVED, WHAT DID A DAY LOOK LIKE IN THE PEOPLE'S LIBRARY?
I ACTUALLY THINK THAT THE LIBRARY WAS ONE OF THE WORKING GROUPS WHERE THERE PROBABLY IS MORE OF LIKE, "THIS IS AN EVERYDAY THING."
ZL: ONCE IT OPENED FOR THE DAY THINGS KIND OF JUST FLOWED BASED ON WHAT WAS NEEDED AT THE MOMENT...
AND HOW MANY PEOPLE WERE THERE...

ZL: WE WOULD BEGIN SHELVING BOOKS AND RESHELVING BOOKS.

CREATING NEW TOPICS AND BINS WHEN IT WAS NEEDED.

ZL: WE'D WRITE "OWSL" IN MAGIC MARKER SO THAT IT WAS CLEAR THAT IT WAS A LIBRARY BOOK AND NOT SOMEBODY'S PERSONAL BOOK.
OWSL
WE'D ALSO PUT A LITTLE STICKER ON THE BACK OF IT TO SHOW OURSELVES THAT WE HAD CATALOGED IT...
AND THEN IT WOULD GET SHELVED IN THE APPROPRIATE BIN.
BUT THEN ALL OF THOSE SHEETS OF PAPER WITH THE ISBN NUMBERS, AT THE END OF THE NIGHT...
YOU KNOW, THIS WOULD SHIFT DEPENDING ON THE NIGHT...
SOMEBODY WOULD USUALLY TAKE THEM HOME WHO WASN'T SLEEPING IN THE PARK AND ENTER ALL OF THEM INTO LIBRARYTHING...
WHICH IS WHAT WE WERE USING FOR THE CATALOG.

SOUNDS LIKE THE WORK WAS SIMILAR TO A PUBLIC LIBRARY, BUT HOW DID PEOPLE CHECK OUT BOOKS?

IF YOU WANTED TO TAKE A BOOK, WE TRUSTED THAT YOU WOULD EITHER BRING IT BACK WHEN YOU WERE DONE,

OR YOU WOULD PASS IT ALONG TO SOMEBODY ELSE,

OR IF YOU REALLY NEED THAT BOOK THEN IT HAD FOUND WHERE IT BELONGED.

ALSO A LOT
OF THE STUFF WE
DID WAS FRONTLINE
REFERENCE WORK.
SOMEBODY
WOULD COME
INTO THE LIBRARY
AND THEY'D SAY,
ZL: "I'M INTERESTED
IN PERMACULTURE."
"I'M INTERESTED
IN FEMINISM."
"I'M INTERESTED
IN QUEER THEORY,
WHAT DO YOU
HAVE?"

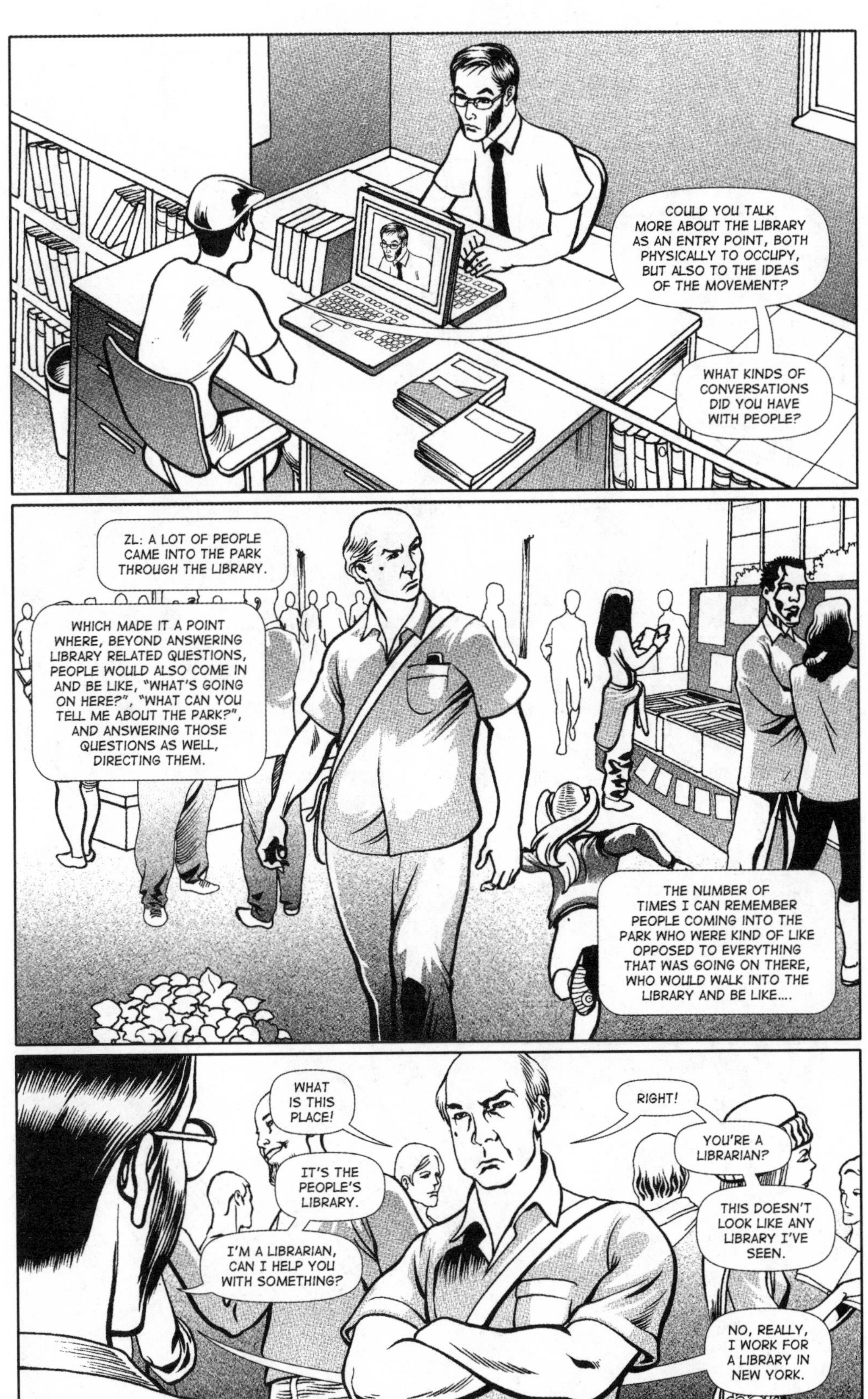
COULD YOU TALK MORE ABOUT THE LIBRARY AS AN ENTRY POINT, BOTH PHYSICALLY TO OCCUPY, BUT ALSO TO THE IDEAS OF THE MOVEMENT?
WHAT KINDS OF CONVERSATIONS DID YOU HAVE WITH PEOPLE?
ZL: A LOT OF PEOPLE CAME INTO THE PARK THROUGH THE LIBRARY.
WHICH MADE IT A POINT WHERE, BEYOND ANSWERING LIBRARY RELATED QUESTIONS, PEOPLE WOULD ALSO COME IN AND BE LIKE, "WHAT'S GOING ON HERE?", "WHAT CAN YOU TELL ME ABOUT THE PARK?", AND ANSWERING THOSE QUESTIONS AS WELL, DIRECTING THEM.
THE NUMBER OF TIMES I CAN REMEMBER PEOPLE COMING INTO THE PARK WHO WERE KIND OF LIKE OPPOSED TO EVERYTHING THAT WAS GOING ON THERE, WHO WOULD WALK INTO THE LIBRARY AND BE LIKE....
WHAT IS THIS PLACE!
IT'S THE PEOPLE'S LIBRARY.
I'M A LIBRARIAN, CAN I HELP YOU WITH SOMETHING?
RIGHT!
YOU'RE A LIBRARIAN?
THIS DOESN'T LOOK LIKE ANY LIBRARY I'VE SEEN.
NO, REALLY, I WORK FOR A LIBRARY IN NEW YORK.

Free Books
fiction
LET ME KNOW IF YOU HAVE ANY QUESTIONS.
TAKE A BOOK IF YOU FIND SOMETHING YOU LIKE.
ZL: I THINK IT JUST FLEW IN THE FACE OF PEOPLE'S EXPECTATIONS AND I THINK IT SHOWED THEM THAT IT WASN'T JUST THIS AIMLESS ACTION...
THE ACT OF OCCUPATION AND THE ACT OF BUILDING THIS ALTERNATIVE SPACE, IN SOME WAYS IT WASN'T ABOUT THE DEMAND....
IT WAS ABOUT SHOWING THAT WE CAN TAKE CARE OF EACH OTHER.
SHOWING WHAT WE CAN DO.
I THINK WE WERE REALLY DOING MUTUAL AID IN PRACTICE.

ZL: SOME OF THAT TYPE OF STUFF WAS REALLY WHAT HAD A LASTING IMPRESSION ON THEM.
HERE
LIBRARY
YOU CAN SAY THAT OCCUPY DIDN'T HAVE DEMANDS...
OR THAT PERSON OVER THERE HAS A CRAZY SIGN...
BUT PEOPLE CAME AND THEY COULD GO INTO A REALLY IMPRESSIVELY STOCKED LIBRARY AND GET HELP FINDING WHAT THEY WERE LOOKING FOR.
IF PEOPLE WERE HUNGRY...
THEY WERE FED...
OR THEY COULD GET BASIC MEDICAL SERVICES.
AS AN ENTRY POINT INTO THE PARK I THINK THAT ONE OF THE THINGS THAT THE LIBRARY DID IS FROM THE OUTSET OF COMING IN...
IT CHALLENGED PEOPLE'S PRECONCEIVED NOTIONS ABOUT WHAT THE PARK WAS.

WHAT DID YOU PERSONALLY TAKE AWAY FROM WORKING IN THE PEOPLE'S LIBRARY?
IT ALWAYS SOUNDS SILLY TO SAY AND IT'S HARD TO TRANSLATE CERTAIN EXPERIENCES AND CERTAIN EMOTIONS INTO CLEAR WORDS.
BUT THERE WERE MOMENTS IN THE PARK WHERE GIVING SOMEBODY A BOOK FELT LIKE THIS AMAZING RADICAL THING TO DO.
IT WAS A TRANSFORMATIVE MOMENT THAT I'M HANDING THIS PERSON A BOOK.
ZL: I HAND PEOPLE BOOKS ALL THE TIME, BUT THERE, AT TIMES, GIVING SOMEBODY A BOOK, THAT WAS A REVOLUTION.
THE MEMORY OF THAT FEELING IS ONE OF THE THINGS THAT WE'VE REALLY LOST IN THE TIME SINCE.
I DO A LOT OF THIS STUFF AT MY DAY JOB AND THEN THERE I WAS DOING THIS STUFF IN THE FREE TIME I HAD.
BUT IN ONE CASE I WOULDN'T HAVE BEEN THERE UNLESS YOU WERE PAYING ME AND IN THE OTHER CASE AS SOON AS I COULD GET THERE, I WAS THERE.

ZL: BECAUSE, LOOK, IN THE AFTERMATH OF OCCUPY A LOT OF IMPORTANT ISSUES HAD BEEN BROUGHT UP CORRECTLY. HOWEVER...
OCCUPY WAS NOT GOOD ON RACE,
OCCUPY WAS NOT GOOD ON GENDER,
OCCUPY WAS NOT GOOD ON A LOT OF SAFETY ISSUES AT TIMES,
OCCUPY BY ITS AMORPHOUSNESS AT TIMES ALLOWED ITSELF TO BE A SPACE WHERE THE RADICAL RIGHT WAS MOVING IN.
THERE ARE A LOT OF ISSUES WITH OCCUPY.
BUT ONE OF THE LESSONS I'VE TAKEN AWAY IS WHAT WORKED IN OCCUPY.
IN MY EXPERIENCE PEOPLE ALL ARE WILLING TO GO OFF AT LENGTH AND BASH THE GENERAL ASSEMBLY...
I'LL BE HONEST, I DID NOT LIKE GENERAL ASSEMBLY MEETINGS.
I USUALLY WOULDN'T GO.
BECAUSE THOSE WERE ALSO ALIENATING.

ZL: BUT PEOPLE DON'T BASH THE KITCHEN.
PEOPLE DON'T BASH THE MEDICAL TEAM.
PEOPLE DON'T BASH THE LIBRARY.

SO ONE OF THE THINGS THAT I'VE TAKEN AWAY IS THAT MUTUAL AID REALLY WORKS...
AND MUTUAL AID IS REALLY TRANSFORMATIVE.

BOOK
LIBRARY
DONATIONS
WHEN PEOPLE FEEL THE AID AND THE MUTUAL PART OF IT THERE IS SOMETHING IN THAT EXPERIENCE WHICH IS VERY DIFFERENT AND VERY POWERFUL FROM THE FEELING OF ALIENATION THAT MOST OF US EXPERIENCE IN OUR DAILY LIVES AND AT OUR REGULAR JOBS.

THAT'S REALLY INTERESTING.
I DON'T THINK MOST PEOPLE WOULD VIEW OCCUPY AS A KIND OF PRACTICE IN MUTUAL AID.
DO YOU HAVE ANY FINAL POINTS?
THE THING THAT I WOULD EMPHASIZE IS, AGAIN, WHAT YOU REALLY CARRY WITH YOU AFTER PARTICIPATING IN SOMETHING LIKE OCCUPY IS IT DOESN'T MATTER HOW MANY BOOKS YOU HAVE READ DESCRIBING WHAT THE WORLD COULD BE LIKE.
YOU FEEL WHAT IT COULD BE LIKE AND ONCE YOU'VE HAD THE EXPERIENCE THAT IS ALWAYS GOING TO INFORM YOU GOING AHEAD.
GENDER STUDIES
LIBRARY
FOR ME, OCCUPY WAS REALLY AN EXAMPLE OF NOT JUST MODELING THE WORLD WE WANT TO LIVE IN, BUT ACTIVELY BUILDING IT.

I SPOKE WITH ZACHARY EARLIER AND WAS HOPING YOU MIGHT EXPAND OUR CONVERSATION AND TALK ABOUT THE LIBRARY'S WORKING GROUP.
JAIME T. (JT) LIBRARIAN AT OCCUPY WALL STREET
SURE, FIRST IT'S IMPORTANT TO POINT OUT WE TOOK AUTONOMY SERIOUSLY.
JT: THE AUTONOMY OF THE WORKING GROUP VIS-À-VIS THE REST OF OCCUPY WAS CRUCIAL, AND ALSO INDIVIDUAL AUTONOMY WITHIN THE GROUP.
SO FOR EXAMPLE WE WERE THE LAST GROUP THAT JOINED UP TO THE FINANCE-WORKING GROUP WHEN THAT BECAME MORE CENTRALIZED.

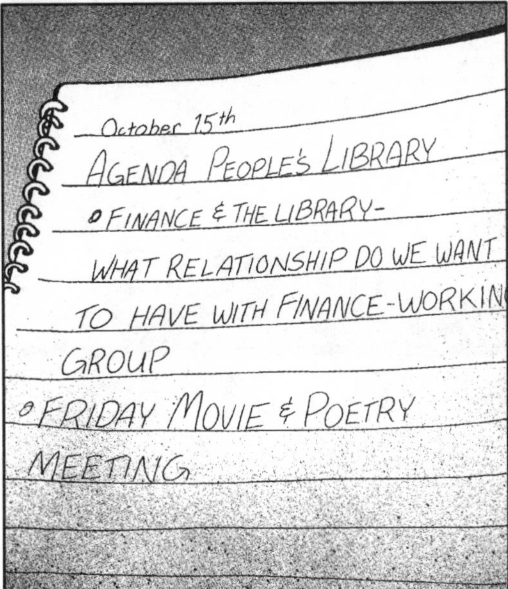
October 15th
Agenda People's Library
○ Finance & the Library-
What relationship do we want
to have with Finance-workin
group
○ Friday Movie & Poetry
Meeting

ANYTHING TO ADD TO THE AGENDA?

OK, FIRST ITEM IS OUR RELATIONSHIP TO FINANCE.
UMM...
LET'S SEE...
I HAVE JAIME FIRST ON STACK.

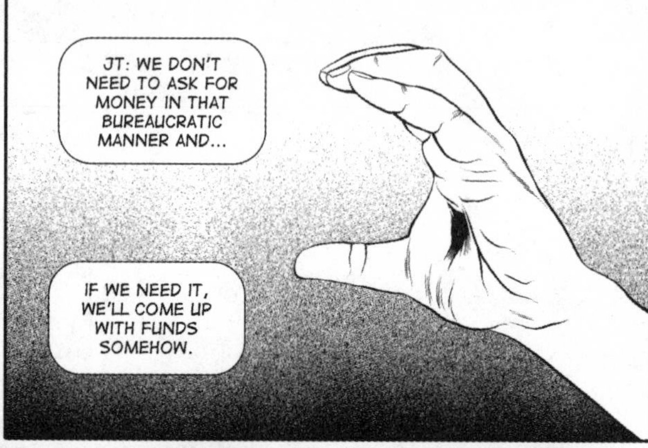

WE EVENTUALLY CAME TO A CONSENSUS ON JOINING.

BUT IT WAS DISCUSSED FOR SOME TIME.

DOES THAT MAKE SENSE?
SO AS THE LIBRARY-WORKING GROUP WE TOOK OUR AUTONOMY FROM THE LARGER OCCUPY MOVEMENT SERIOUSLY.
BUT EVEN WITHIN THE WORKING GROUP ITSELF,
AND AS CLOSE AS WE ALL WERE,
WE ALSO TOOK INDIVIDUAL AUTONOMY SERIOUSLY. FOR EXAMPLE, IF THERE WAS A PROJECT THAT SOMEONE WANTED TO DO IN THE LIBRARY,
LIBRARY
THAT WASN'T GOING TO INTERRUPT THE GENERAL WORK OF THE LIBRARY... WE WERE LIKE, *"YEAH, SURE, GO DO IT."*
"WE'RE BEHIND YOU."
PEOPLE WERE ABLE TO TAKE OFF AND RUN WITH THINGS THAT THEY WANTED TO DO.
THERE WERE NO BOSSES IN THE WORKING GROUPS, IT RAN HORIZONTALLY.
WHAT IS THE PURVIEW OF THE LARGER GROUP?
WHAT ARE THE GROUP'S ACTUAL RESPONSIBILITIES AND WHAT ARE OUR RESPONSIBILITIES TO IT?
SO MAINTAINING AUTONOMY BY ONLY TAKING TO THE WORKING GROUP MEETINGS WHAT HAS TO BE APPROVED BY THE WORKING GROUP
I THINK WAS REALLY IMPORTANT.
DOES THAT MAKE SENSE?

YEAH, SORT OF. COULD YOU MAYBE TALK ME THROUGH IT IN MORE DETAIL?
SURE, FOR US ANY EXPENDITURES OF MONEY OR ANYTHING THAT WOULD DISRUPT THE WORK OF THE LIBRARY,
LIKE NEEDING A LARGE AMOUNT OF SPACE OR NEEDING OTHER PEOPLE'S HELP OR...
JT: BRINGING UP PROBLEMS THAT HAD GOTTEN TOO LARGE FOR ONE OR TWO PEOPLE TO HANDLE BY THEMSELVES.
AT ONE POINT WE HAD THIS MAN COMING DOWN ON THE WEEKENDS AND WORKING WITH THE LIBRARY.
WE AT FIRST THOUGHT HE WAS JUST A GRUMPY PERSON...
BUT QUICKLY IT BECAME CLEAR THAT HE WAS ACTUALLY UNSTABLE.

JT: CERTAIN CONVERSATIONS PEOPLE WERE HAVING WITH HIM WHERE THERE WOULD BE SOME CONFLICT.
WHAT! WHAT! DON'T MOVE THAT BOOK!
IT WAS OFTEN UNRESOLVABLE AND DIDN'T FEEL LIKE HE WAS TRYING.
THAT DOESN'T GO THERE!!
DON'T TOUCH MY SECTION.
THAT WAS SOMETHING THAT BECAME A PROBLEM THAT WAS TOO BIG FOR ONE PERSON.
WE ALL NEEDED TO WORK TOGETHER TO FIX OR DO SOMETHING ABOUT IT WITHIN THE WORKING GROUP.
SO THOSE ARE SOME ISSUES WE DEALT WITH IN THE WORKING GROUP.

JT: ONE THING ABOUT THE OCCUPATION THAT BECAME VERY APPARENT TO ME AFTER I GOT INVOLVED WAS THAT HERE IN NEW YORK THERE ARE ALL OF THESE INDIVIDUALS IN VERY SMALL GROUPS PARALLELING EACH OTHER AND DOING VERY SIMILAR THINGS...
OR AT LEAST SIMILAR POLITICS OR COMPLEMENTARY PROJECTS.
PEOPLE HAVE BEEN IN THE SAME NEIGHBORHOOD AND DIDN'T KNOW EACH OTHER AND DIDN'T WORK WITH EACH OTHER.
THE OCCUPATION, BY EXISTING IN ONE PHYSICAL SPACE IN CLOSE CONTACT FOR TWO MONTHS AND HAVING TO WORK TOGETHER EVERYDAY, IT BECAME THIS CLEARINGHOUSE IN THE NEW YORK LEFT BASICALLY.
NOW WE ALL KNOW EACH OTHER AND NOT JUST IN PASSING.

JT: FOR ME, ONE OF MY MAIN SOCIAL CIRCLES IN NEW YORK IS PEOPLE I MET THROUGH THE OCCUPATION.
ZACHARY, HE AND I GET BEERS TOGETHER EVERY COUPLE WEEKS.
HOW MANY PEOPLE HAVE ROOMMATES FROM THE OCCUPATION OR ARE WORKING ON OTHER ACTIVISTS' PROJECTS TOGETHER?
I THINK THE MAJOR MISTAKE THAT THE STATE AND CAPITAL MADE IS LETTING US GET TO KNOW EACH OTHER,
ALLOWING US THAT SPACE BECAUSE THEY CAN'T UNDO IT AT THIS POINT.
THEY REALLY CAN'T AND THAT'S IMPORTANT.

Chapter 5

Barcelona to Greensboro

OCCUPY IS A VERY INTERESTING EXAMPLE OF MUTUAL AID, BUT ARE THERE OTHER HISTORICAL EXAMPLES OF THIS SPONTANEITY?
EVERYTHING YOU CAN THINK OF.
NC: I JUST CAME BACK FROM GREENSBORO, NORTH CAROLINA.
Richmond
Virginia Beach
Greensboro
Raleigh
Knoxville
Charlotte
Greenville
Columbia
Atlanta
A SMALL TOWN WITH A FAMOUS HISTORY.
David Richmond
Franklin McCain
Ezell Blair, Jr
IN 1960, FOUR STUDENTS FROM A COLLEGE IN GREENSBORO DECIDED TO SIT IN AT A LUNCH COUNTER AT A WOOLWORTH'S STORE WHERE BLACKS WERE NOT ALLOWED.
WELL, THEY WERE ARRESTED, OF COURSE, AND TREATED PRETTY BRUTALLY.

NC: A COUPLE OF OTHERS CAME ALONG...

AND PRETTY SOON...

YOU HAVE THE CIVIL RIGHTS MOVEMENT.

NC: THE CIVIL RIGHTS MOVEMENT WAS A MOVEMENT OF SOLIDARITY AND MUTUAL SUPPORT.

FREEDOM BUSES, THE SELMA MARCH...
THE WHOLE THING WAS JUST...
BLACK CHURCHES AND SOME WHITES FROM THE NORTH JOINED IN.

THESE WERE VERY DANGEROUS.
PEOPLE GETTING KILLED.

BUT THERE WAS A BIG SPONTANEOUS MOVEMENT OF MUTUAL AID.
I WAS DOWN IN THE SOUTH IN CIVIL RIGHTS DEMONSTRATIONS, IT WAS INCREDIBLE.
THAT IS WHAT HAPPENS WHEN PEOPLE ARE LIBERATED A LITTLE BIT.

WHAT HAPPENED IN GREENSBORO IS KIND OF LIKE THE OCCUPY MOVEMENT.
NC: WHEN THE OCCUPY MOVEMENT STARTED IT WAS SPONTANEOUS.
NOBODY EXPECTED IT TO GO ANYWHERE, INCLUDING THE PARTICIPANTS.
BUT IT JUST LIT A SPARK.
PEOPLE WERE WAITING FOR IT SOMEHOW AND THEY JOINED IN AND DID THE SAME THING.

IT'S HAPPENING ALL OVER THE HEMISPHERE,

IT DOESN'T GET REPORTED BECAUSE IT IS TOO DANGEROUS.

NC: IN QUEBEC, FOR EXAMPLE, THAT'S RIGHT NEXT DOOR,

THERE ARE HUGE DEMONSTRATIONS EVERY NIGHT [2012]...

YOU KNOW, HUNDRED OF THOUSANDS OF PEOPLE. IT STARTED WITH A STUDENT STRIKE.

IT'S NOW BEEN BROUGHT INTO THE CITY. THEY'RE CONDEMNING THE NEO-LIBERAL POLICIES AND ALL KINDS OF THINGS, REALLY MAJOR, MAJOR EVENTS.

DEHORS LES NÉOLIBÉRAUX

WOULD BARCELONA IN THE '30s ALSO BE AN EXAMPLE?
TAKE A LOOK AT BARCELONA IN THE '30s.

NC: THAT'S REGARDED AS SPONTANEOUS AND IN A SENSE IT WAS BUT WHAT'S FORGOTTEN IS THAT IT FOLLOWED ABOUT 30 YEARS OF FREE EDUCATION...

FREE SCHOOLS, ANARCHIST ORGANIZING, COMMUNITY ORGANIZING...

EFFORTS TO TAKE OVER COMMUNITIES...

AND FREE THEM UP, WHICH WERE DESTROYED BY VIOLENCE.

BY THE TIME YOU GOT TO 1936 IT WAS IN EVERYONE'S HEAD.

SO WHEN THE OPPORTUNITY CAME THEY JUST KNEW WHAT TO DO.

Chapter 6

Student Loan Debt

PROFESSOR, I WOULD LIKE TO GET YOUR THOUGHTS ON THE WORK BEING DONE POST-OCCUPY?
I'VE FOUND ESPECIALLY INSPIRING THE ORGANIZING AROUND STUDENT LOAN DEBT WITH GROUPS LIKE STRIKE DEBT AND ROLLING JUBILEE.
THIS HITS HOME, 'CAUSE, WELL...
MY PARTNER AND I OWE...
UMM, $200,000 IN STUDENT LOANS.
THIS DEBT JUST WEIGHS ON US...
IT'S INCREDIBLE...
IT CREATES THIS SITUATION IN WHICH...
YOU'RE A SLAVE.
AND IT'S FOR THE REST OF YOUR LIFE.

YEAH, WE HAVE TO FIGURE OUT HOW TO PAY THIS DEBT OURSELVES. IT'S VERY SCARY.
RRRRIIIIIINNGG
RRRRIIIIIINNGG
BRRREEEEEEEEP
THAT IS EXACTLY THE POINT. IF YOU DON'T CONTROL PEOPLE, IF THEY ARE FREE, THEY CAN CAUSE YOU TROUBLE.
BUT THIS WAY YOUNG PEOPLE ARE TRAPPED FOR THE REST OF THEIR LIVES.
IF A BUSINESS CAN'T DEAL WITH ITS LOANS, IT CAN GO BANKRUPT AND START OVER.
YOU CAN'T DO THAT WITH STUDENT LOANS.
FURTHERMORE THEY CAN GARNISH YOUR SOCIAL SECURITY. YOU'RE TRAPPED FOR LIFE.
I CALL IT GANGSTER.
RDDRDDDRRRRRR
THERE IS NO ECONOMIC REASON WHY A COLLEGE EDUCATION CAN'T BE FREE.

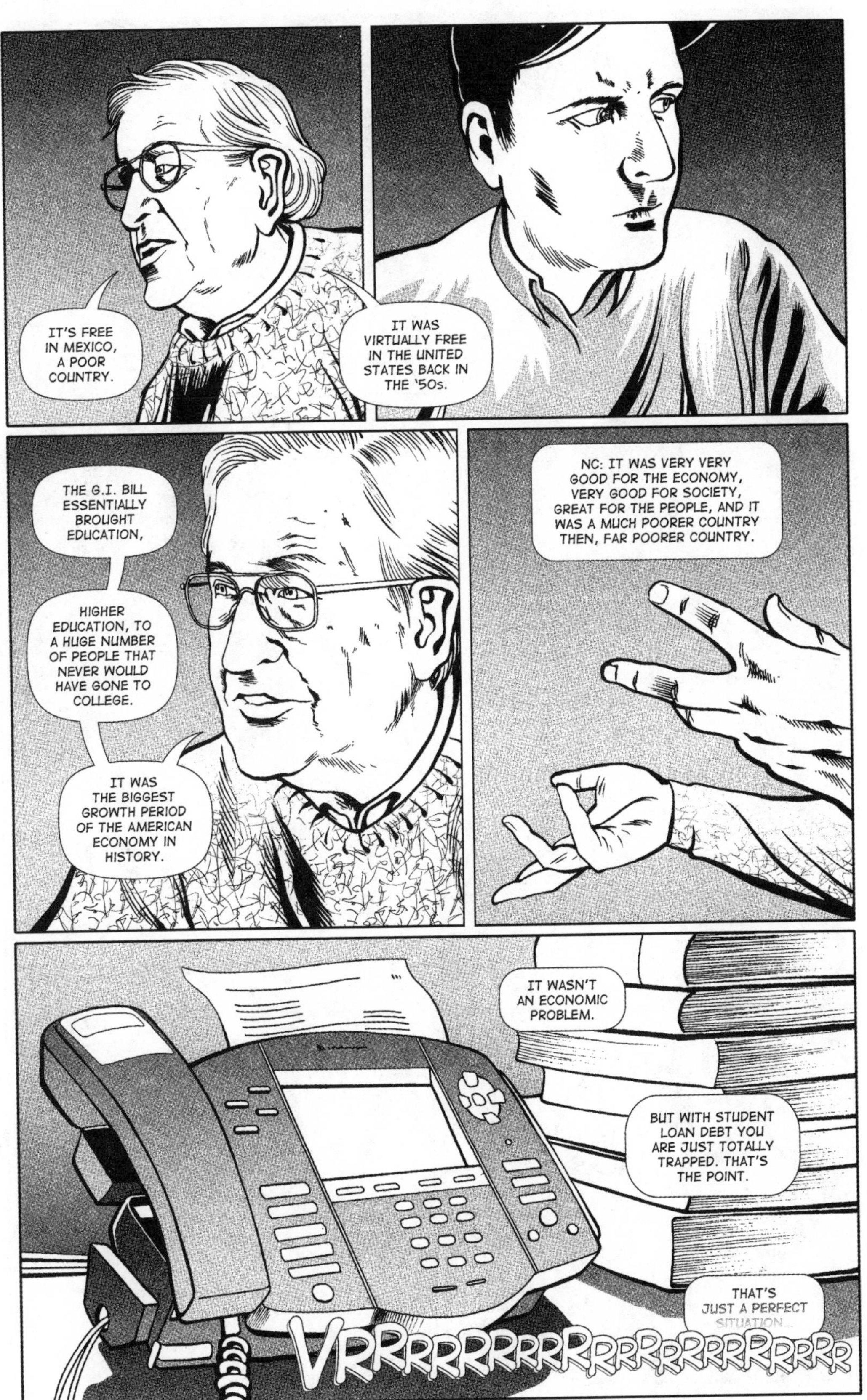
IT'S FREE IN MEXICO, A POOR COUNTRY.
IT WAS VIRTUALLY FREE IN THE UNITED STATES BACK IN THE '50s.
THE G.I. BILL ESSENTIALLY BROUGHT EDUCATION,
HIGHER EDUCATION, TO A HUGE NUMBER OF PEOPLE THAT NEVER WOULD HAVE GONE TO COLLEGE.
IT WAS THE BIGGEST GROWTH PERIOD OF THE AMERICAN ECONOMY IN HISTORY.
NC: IT WAS VERY VERY GOOD FOR THE ECONOMY, VERY GOOD FOR SOCIETY, GREAT FOR THE PEOPLE, AND IT WAS A MUCH POORER COUNTRY THEN, FAR POORER COUNTRY.
IT WASN'T AN ECONOMIC PROBLEM.
BUT WITH STUDENT LOAN DEBT YOU ARE JUST TOTALLY TRAPPED. THAT'S THE POINT.
THAT'S JUST A PERFECT SITUATION...
VRRRRRRRRRRRRRRRRRRRR

JW: AS THE FAX MACHINE DROWNED OUT CHOMSKY'S POINT, MY THOUGHTS DRIFTED TO AN EXPERIENCED FILMMAKER AND WRITER ASTRA TAYLOR HAD AT OCCUPY.
STEP RIGHT UP, STEP RIGHT UP! HOW MUCH DO YOU OWE? COME AND TELL US HOW VALUABLE YOU REALLY ARE TO THE ONE PERCENT.
70,000
80,000
ASTRA TAYLOR
42,000
80,000
DAMN STUDENT LOANS!
40,000

YOU'RE A SLAVE AND IT'S FOR THE REST OF YOUR LIFE.
YOU'RE A SLAVE AND IT'S FOR THE REST OF YOUR LIFE.
YOU'RE A SLAVE AND IT'S FOR THE REST OF YOUR LIFE.
CHOMSKY'S NOT WRONG. I DON'T EVEN THINK HE'S BEING MEAN.
BUT THESE WORDS ARE HAUNTING ME STILL AFTER THE INTERVIEW.
I NEED TO TALK WITH OTHERS ABOUT STUDENT DEBT.
WHAT IS THIS SLAVERY MANY OTHERS AND I ARE IN?
HOW CAN I BREAK THESE BONDS?
JW: I DECIDED TO TALK WITH PROFESSOR GEORGE CAFFENTZIS.
call:
George Caffentzis
HE WAS INVOLVED IN THE EARLY FORMATION OF STRIKE DEBT AND ROLLING JUBILEE.
PROFESSOR GEORGE CAFFENTZIS (GC)

I SPOKE WITH CHOMSKY A FEW MONTHS AGO AND WE DISCUSSED STUDENT LOAN DEBT.
HE NOTED THE WAYS IT CREATES A TYPE OF SLAVERY.
I'M INTERESTED IN TALKING WITH YOU IN MORE DEPTH ABOUT THE RELATIONSHIP BETWEEN DEBT AND WORK. AND ALSO HOW STUDENT LOAN DEBT IS DIFFERENT FROM OTHER FORMS OF DEBT.

WELL, THERE ARE MANY DIFFERENT FORMS OF DEBT AND MANY DIFFERENCES AMONG THEM.
THE MOST IMPORTANT IS SOMETHING I CALL PROFIT DEBT VERSUS USE-VALUE DEBT.

$
BANK
$
GC: MOST DEBT THAT GOES ON IN A SOCIETY IS PROFIT DEBT, WHICH IS ONE CAPITALIST, A BANK OR FINANCIAL INSTITUTION, LENDING MONEY TO ANOTHER CAPITALIST.

THAT'S THE KIND OF DEBT THAT HAS BEEN AROUND SINCE THE BEGINNING OF CAPITALISM...
BUT THAT IS NOT THE KIND OF DEBT WE ARE DEALING WITH IN TERMS OF STUDENT LOAN DEBT. IT'S IMPORTANT TO MAKE THAT DISTINCTION BECAUSE SOMETIMES IT GETS CONFUSED.
DIPLOMA
DEBT
DIPLOMA
JOB
THE KIND OF DEBT WE ARE DEALING WITH, WHAT I CALL USE-VALUE DEBT, IS A DEBT THAT PEOPLE INCUR IN ORDER TO GET SOME *VITAL NECESSITY* THAT THEY CAN USE TO LIVE AND MAKE THEIR LIVES BETTER.

WHAT'S BEEN HAPPENING IS THAT UNIVERSITY EDUCATION HAS NOT ONLY BEEN INCREASINGLY PRIVATIZED.
BUT BASICALLY THE MONETARY REQUIREMENTS IN ORDER TO BECOME EDUCATED AT THE HIGHEST LEVEL IN OUR SOCIETY HAVE GONE UP ALMOST EXPONENTIALLY IN THE LAST 30 YEARS.
IT'S A PRODUCT OF PUBLIC UNIVERSITIES BEING DEFUNDED BY STATE LEGISLATURES...
TIK TIK TAK TAK TIK
TIK TAK TAK TIK TAK
SO INCREASINGLY PUBLIC UNIVERSITIES HAVE HAD TO INCREASE THEIR TUITION.
I JUST PULLED UP SOME FIGURES FROM ARIZONA. THE CUTS ARE VERY SEVERE.
UNIVERSITY OF ARIZONA HAS EXPERIENCED DRAMATIC CUTS.
THE FIGURES HERE SAY...
"THE LEGISLATURE [AZ] CUT THIS YEAR [2015] $99 MILLION FROM UNIVERSITIES, $19 MILLION FROM COMMUNITY COLLEGES."
"ARIZONA IS SPENDING 47 PERCENT LESS THIS YEAR PER COLLEGE STUDENT THAN IT DID IN 2008, ADJUSTED FOR INFLATION. THAT'S A LARGER PERCENTAGE CUT THAN ANY OTHER STATE."
"IN RESPONSE TO CUTS, UNIVERSITIES AND COMMUNITY COLLEGES HAVE RAISED TUITION AND FEES."
"ARIZONA [ACCORDING TO CENTER ON BUDGET POLICY PRIORITIES, AZ] HAS SEEN THE GREATEST TUITION INCREASES, RISING 83.6 PERCENT, OR $4,734 PER STUDENT, AFTER ADJUSTING FOR INFLATION, FROM 2008 TO 2015."

GC: YES, THAT'S FINANCIALLY SPEAKING BUT ALSO WE HAVE TO BEGIN TO UNDERSTAND WHAT THIS MEANS IN TERMS OF THE AVERAGE PERSON...
WHO IS NOW FACING ENORMOUS DEBT FOR DOING SOMETHING THAT IN THE PAST WAS PERFECTLY EASY TO DO WITHOUT INCURRING ANY KIND OF SERIOUS DEBT.
THEY BECOME VERY LIMITED IN THEIR CONCEPTION OF WHAT THEY CAN DO IN THE FUTURE.
FOR EXAMPLE, I WENT TO UNIVERSITY IN THE '60s; IT WAS BASICALLY FREE.
YOU CAN DEAL WITH THE ISSUE OF STUDENT LOAN DEBT AS A FINANCIAL PROBLEM, LIKE A MATTER OF ACCOUNTING.
HOW MUCH YOU GET AND HOW MUCH YOU DON'T GET, SO ON AND SO FORTH.
BUT WE HAVE TO REALIZE THAT DEBT IS AN EXTREME DISCIPLINARY TOOL FOR PEOPLE IN OUR SOCIETY.
DEBT IS SOMETHING THAT IS USED IN A WAY TO MAKE PEOPLE BEHAVE.

GC: IT WAS ALWAYS CLEAR TO ME AS A TEACHER WALKING INTO A CLASSROOM THAT NO MATTER HOW GOOD YOU ARE...
YOU FIND STUDENTS DOZING OFF.
WHAT'S GOING ON?
YOU WERE LATE AND FELL ASLEEP.
SORRY, PROFESSOR. JUST CAME OFF THE NIGHT SHIFT AT MY JOB AND I JUST DIDN'T HAVE A CHANCE TO SLEEP.
GC: THIS IS SOMETHING THAT'S VERY COMMON.
IT IS SOMETHING THAT HAS ENTERED INTO THE EVERYDAY LIFE OF PEOPLE AND BEGUN TO LIMIT THEIR POLITICAL POSSIBILITY...
THEIR ABILITY TO ORGANIZE THEMSELVES AND OTHER PEOPLE.

STUDENT DEBT= $40,000.
RENT= $650.
GC: IN A WAY THE CAMPUSES HAVE NOT BEEN THE TYPE OF CENTERS OF DIFFERENT MOVEMENTS IN THE WAYS THEY USED TO BE.

PART OF IT HAS TO DO WITH THE GENERAL DEPRESSION THAT GOES ON IN OUR SOCIETY...
BUT MUCH OF IT HAS TO DO WITH FINANCIALLY DRIVEN DEPOLITICIZATION OF THE CAMPUS.

I THINK IT'S AN IMPORTANT ASPECT OF EDUCATION AND THE CONSEQUENCES OF THIS DEVELOPMENT.
I'M SO TIRED. WONDER WHAT THOSE PEOPLE WERE PROTESTING.
WISH I HAD MORE TIME TO BE INVOLVED.
BASICALLY, STUDENTS GO INTO DEBT FOR TENS OF THOUSANDS OF DOLLARS IN ORDER TO BE EDUCATED.
WHATEVER, I JUST NEED TO FINISH THIS COURSE AND FIND A JOB.
IN THE PROCESS THE EDUCATION ITSELF IS UNDERMINED.

SO, DEBT IMPACTS STUDENTS' WORK WHILE IN UNIVERSITY AND ALSO AFTER, CORRECT?
WHEN STUDENTS LEAVE THE UNIVERSITY, A WAVE OF PAYMENTS FOR STUDENT DEBT FOLLOWS BEHIND YOU LIKE A TIDAL WAVE,
IF I CAN PUT IT IN THAT KIND OF NIGHTMARISH IMAGE.
YOU THEN HAVE TO FIND EMPLOYMENT AS QUICKLY AS POSSIBLE IN PLACES THAT YOU MIGHT FIND POLITICALLY, SOCIALLY OBJECTIONABLE, BUT THERE YOU ARE,
YOU HAVE TO HAVE IT IN ORDER TO PAY OFF YOUR DEBT.
OFTEN STUDENTS WHO, IN THEIR UNIVERSITY YEARS, HAVE A POLITICAL AGENDA ON THEIR MIND, WHEN THEY LEAVE THEY FIND THEMSELVES ALONE,
BASICALLY BURDENED WITH A TREMENDOUS AMOUNT OF DEBT AND LOOKING FOR THE "GOOD JOB."
THIS USUALLY INVOLVES WORKING FOR CORPORATIONS, WHICH THEY HAD PREVIOUSLY BEEN FIGHTING AGAINST WHILE IN SCHOOL.
THIS HAPPENS ALL THE TIME.

IT'S A PART OF THE CONSEQUENCES OF THIS DEBT MACHINE.
SOME PEOPLE ARE CALLING WELFARE "DEBT-FARE." IT'S PART OF YOUR CONTEMPORARY LIFE, I'M AFRAID, JEFF.

I FEEL IT.

I'M $100,000 IN DEBT FROM MY MASTER'S DEGREE, SO...
I...I FEEL THAT TIDAL WAVE.

JEFF, THAT'S TERRIBLE, I'M SO SORRY TO HEAR THAT.
I THINK STUDENT LOAN DEBT HAS BEEN MUCH MORE EFFECTIVE AS AN OPPRESSIVE TOOL...

GC: THAN COPS ON CAMPUS.

Chapter 7

Solidarity

WOULD YOU LIKE SOME MORE TEA?
SURE, YEAH, THAT WOULD BE GREAT, THANKS.
I SPOKE WITH INDIVIDUALS INVOLVED WITH THE PEOPLE'S LIBRARY AT OCCUPY WALL STREET.
ONE OF THEIR MAIN TAKEAWAYS FROM OCCUPY WAS IT PROVIDED A SPACE TO MEET OTHER ACTIVISTS.
I THINK THAT'S CORRECT.
IT'S JUST DANGEROUS TO ALLOW PEOPLE TO GET TOGETHER.

IT'S BASICALLY DESIGNED TO KEEP PEOPLE SEPARATED.

IT DOES IT IN A VERY SPECIAL WAY, BY...

GETTING *YOU* THE INDIVIDUAL TO INTERPRET MEANING IN YOUR LIFE

AS THE NUMBER OF COMMODITIES YOU POSSESS, NOT...

THE PLEASURE OF HELPING OTHERS TO DO SOMETHING.

NEW
THE ATTACK ON PUBLIC SCHOOLS AND ON SOCIAL SECURITY, I THINK, IS PRETTY MUCH THE SAME.
TAKE SOCIAL SECURITY.
NC: SOCIAL SECURITY IS NOT A PROBLEM AT ALL.
IT HAS GOT ITS OWN FUNDING TO BE IN QUITE GOOD SHAPE FOR A COUPLE OF DECADES.
IF IT BECOMES A PROBLEM YOU KNOW YOU CAN TWEAK IT A LITTLE BIT AND GO ON.
MEDICARE IS A PROBLEM, BUT THAT'S 'CAUSE OF THE PRIVATIZED HEALTH CARE SYSTEM.
MEDICARE ITSELF IS VERY EFFICIENT, BUT IT'S GOT TO WORK THROUGH THE PRIVATIZED SYSTEM, WHICH IS HIGHLY INEFFICIENT.
IT HAS HUGE ADMINISTRATIVE EXPENSES-PROFITS, BIG SALARIES, A TON OF BOOKKEEPING, WHICH YOU DON'T HAVE IN ALMOST ANY COUNTRY,
THERE IS ALMOST NO BOOKKEEPING BECAUSE EVERYTHING COMES FROM ONE SOURCE.

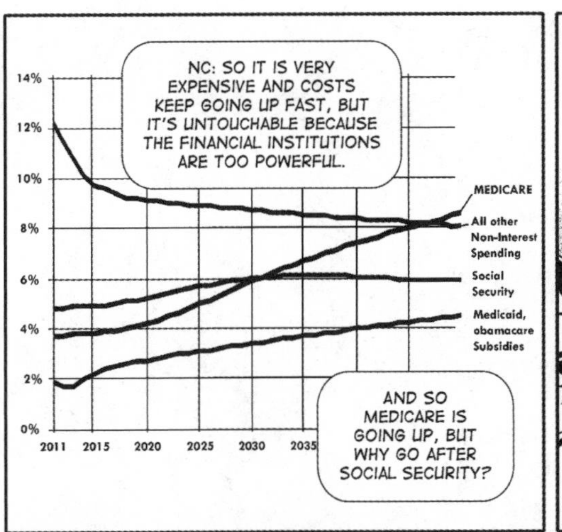
NC: SO IT IS VERY EXPENSIVE AND COSTS KEEP GOING UP FAST, BUT IT'S UNTOUCHABLE BECAUSE THE FINANCIAL INSTITUTIONS ARE TOO POWERFUL.
14%
12%
10%
8%
6%
4%
2%
0%
2011
2015
2020
2025
2030
2035
MEDICARE
All other Non-Interest Spending
Social Security
Medicaid, obamacare Subsidies
AND SO MEDICARE IS GOING UP, BUT WHY GO AFTER SOCIAL SECURITY?

IT'S A PONZI SCHEME.

THE ONLY REASON I CAN—SERIOUS REASON—I CAN THINK OF IS THAT SOCIAL SECURITY IS BASED ON SOLIDARITY.
THAT'S THE PRINCIPLE.
YOU PAY YOUR PAYROLL TAX SO THAT THE LAST GENERATION OF WORKERS CAN LIVE DECENTLY IN THEIR OLD AGE.

AND THE NEXT GENERATION IS SUPPOSED TO DO THE SAME FOR YOU.

ALMOST EVERY DECENT SOCIETY HAS WAYS OF DEALING WITH ELDERLY PEOPLE BECAUSE PEOPLE GET OLD.
THERE IS A POINT WHEN THEY CAN'T WORK ANYMORE.
SO IT COULD BE EXTENDED FAMILIES, MAYBE IT IS THE TRIBE, WHATEVER IT IS...
A VILLAGE, YOU KNOW, PEOPLE JUST DO IT. SUPPORT A LIFE.

NC: BUT WE HAVE TO DRIVE THAT OUT OF PEOPLE'S HEADS.
'CAUSE THE IDEA THAT YOU SHOULD CARE ABOUT SOMEONE ELSE IS VERY DANGEROUS.
YOU ARE SUPPOSED TO BE A MANIAC WHO CARES FOR NOTHING BUT YOURSELF, THAT IS THE IDEAL.
THERE HAVE BEEN MAJOR EFFORTS TO DRIVE THAT INTO PEOPLE'S HEADS.
YOU'RE NOT SUPPOSED TO CARE ABOUT THE DISABLED WIDOW ACROSS TOWN.
YOU ARE SUPPOSED TO BE AN AYN RAND FANATIC.
TAKE CARE OF YOURSELF,
LOOK AFTER NUMBER ONE...
NONE OF YOUR BUSINESS IF ANYONE ELSE NEEDS SOMETHING.

IF YOU TAKE A LOOK AT THE SO-CALLED LIBERTARIANS, IN MY VIEW,
MAYBE AS INDIVIDUALS THEY MAY BE PERFECTLY SINCERE,
BUT WHAT THEIR POSITION ESSENTIALLY ADVOCATES IS CORPORATE TYRANNY.
NC: TAKE A LOOK AT THE REALLY SERIOUS ONES LIKE MURRAY ROTHBARD. THEY SAY...
TOLL
"WHY SHOULD I PAY FOR A ROAD THAT I'M NOT GOING TO USE?"
"IF I WANT A ROAD I'LL BUY IT. I'LL BUILD IT AND I'LL MAKE A TOLL ROAD SO THAT IF ANYONE ELSE WANTS TO USE IT THEY'LL HAVE TO PAY ME."
IT'S AS IF YOU ARE INVENTING A SOCIETY, WHICH WOULD BE BASED ON HATE AND FEAR AND, YOU KNOW, ABSOLUTELY A KIND OF SAVAGERY.
I DON'T WANT TO SAY SAVAGERY BECAUSE PRIMITIVE SOCIETIES ARE NOT LIKE THAT.
THIS GOES WAY BACK INCIDENTALLY TO THE MAGNA CARTA. ACTUALLY THERE WERE TWO CHARTERS IN THE MAGNA CARTA.
THE COMMONS WERE THE BIG AREA OF THE COUNTRY THAT WAS OPEN TO THE POPULATION. THAT'S WHAT THE POPULATION USED FOR SUSTENANCE.
ONE OF THEM WAS CALLED THE CHARTER OF LIBERTIES, THAT'S THE ONE WE TALK ABOUT. THE OTHER WAS THE CHARTER OF THE FOREST. IT WAS CALLED "FOREST," BUT THEY MEANT THE COMMONS.
FOR WOOD, FOR ENERGY, FOR FOOD, YOU KNOW, THEY CULTIVATED IT JOINTLY. PEOPLES' WORK CREATED THE FORESTS.
FORESTS AREN'T JUST WILDERNESS, THEY WERE NURTURED BY PEOPLE IN COMMON.

IN FACT, THE LEGEND OF ROBIN HOOD, THE REASON IT'S POPULAR IS BECAUSE HE WAS DEFENDING THE COMMONS AGAINST THE NOBLES, THE SHERIFF AND ALL THAT STUFF.
THAT KIND OF DISAPPEARED FROM SIGHT.
THE STANDARD VIEW TODAY IS WHAT'S CALLED THE TRAGEDY OF THE COMMONS, GARRETT HARDIN.
IT MEANS IF YOU LEAVE SOMETHING NOT OWNED IT'S GOING TO DISAPPEAR.
THAT'S TRUE IF EVERYBODY IS AN INDIVIDUALIST SAVAGE, LIKE IF YOU DON'T CARE ABOUT ANYONE ELSE THEN ANYTHING THAT IS COMMON, YOU'LL JUST ROB.
IN ANY DECENT SOCIETY IT'S UNTHINKABLE. IN FEUDAL SOCIETIES, INDIGENOUS SOCIETIES, AND TRADITIONAL SOCIETIES WHAT'S COMMON...
IS WHAT WE ALL OWN AND WORK ON AND TAKE CARE OF...
AND TRANSMIT TO THE NEXT GENERATION AND IMPROVE AND SO ON AND SO FORTH.

BUT YOU'VE GOT TO JUST DRIVE THAT IDEA OUT OF PEOPLE'S HEADS.
IT STARTED WITH THE ENCLOSURE MOVEMENT IN ENGLAND, 16TH CENTURY.
DRIVE THE PEOPLE OFF THE LAND AND PRIVATIZE IT.
THE CONCEPT OF PROPERTY THAT YOU GET IN JOHN LOCKE AND OTHERS IS ESSENTIALLY THE SAME.
UNLESS THINGS ARE OWNED, THEY'RE GONNA BE DESTROYED. EVERYTHING HAS TO BE OWNED. YOU READ, SAY, BLACKSTONE, THE GREAT LEGAL THEORIST OF ENGLAND.
HE SAYS, "WELL, AIR AND WATER HAVE TO BE HELD IN COMMON, BUT EVERYTHING ELSE HAS TO BE COMMODIFIED. LAND, YOU KNOW, ENERGY AND FIRE AND SO ON, IT'S ALL GOT TO BE COMMODIFIED."
AND THAT'S A BIG CHANGE FROM ANY KNOWN SOCIETY.
THAT'S THE WESTERN CAPITALIST MARKET SOCIETY, WHICH IS EXTREMELY DESTRUCTIVE.

NC: THAT'S WHY WE ARE DESTROYING THE ENVIRONMENT.
IF WE CAN HAVE TAR SANDS AND SHALE OIL, WE'LL BE OK FOR ANOTHER HUNDRED YEARS, MEANWHILE...
OUR GRANDCHILDREN WILL BE LIVING ON MOUNTAINTOPS,
BUT THAT'S NOT OUR BUSINESS BECAUSE WE DON'T WANT TO THINK ABOUT THINGS LIKE THIS.

Chapter 8

Conclusion

TIME'S UP.

OK, THANKS.

PROFESSOR, COULD I ASK YOU JUST ONE MORE QUESTION?
DO YOU THINK THE WORKPLACE TAKEOVERS OF FACTORIES, LIKE IN ARGENTINA, MIGHT BE A MODEL THAT COULD WORK IN THIS COUNTRY?

SURE, THERE ARE SOME VERY CONCRETE EXAMPLES.
I HAVE TALKED ABOUT THEM BEFORE.
TAKE THE AUTO INDUSTRY.

NC: IT WAS BASICALLY NATIONALIZED, WHEN OBAMA TOOK IT OVER.
GM
WELL, THERE ARE A COUPLE OF THINGS YOU COULD DO ONCE IT WAS NATIONALIZED.
ONE IS WHAT THEY DID DO...
RESTRUCTURE IT AND HAND IT BACK TO THE OLD OWNERS OR PEOPLE VERY MUCH LIKE THEM AND LET IT KEEP DOING WHAT IT WAS DOING BEFORE.
THAT'S ONE POSSIBILITY.
ANOTHER POSSIBILITY WOULD BE TO HAND IT OVER TO THE WORKFORCE AND THE COMMUNITIES AND SUPPORT THEM IN PRODUCING THINGS THE COUNTRY REALLY NEEDS.

PROFESSOR CHOMSKY, THANK YOU AGAIN FOR TAKING THE TIME TO TALK WITH ME.
IT'S BEEN REALLY EYE OPENING.
YOU'RE WELCOME.

NOTES

PAGE 11

Robinson, P., "The Chomsky Problem," *The New York Times,* February 25, 1979.

PAGE 16

Panel 4: Chomsky, N., & Otero, C. *Language and Politics, expanded 2nd ed.* (Oakland, CA: AK Press, 2004), p. 113.

PAGE 17

Panel 1: Chomsky, N., "Language and Freedom" in Pateman, B. (ed.), *Chomsky on Anarchism* (Oakland, CA: AK Press, 2005), p. 115.

Panels 2 and 3: Chomsky, N., & Peck, J., *The Chomsky Reader* (London: Serpent's Tail, 1995), p. 149. Wilhelm von Humboldt quote can also be found in Humboldt, W.V., & Burrow, J. W., *The Limits of State Action* (London: Cambridge University Press, 1969).

*Chomsky does offer a cautionary note in *Language and Politics* connecting ideas of human nature with those of freedom. He does not want to over state a connection between human nature and the organization of society. He states, "The most that one can do, I think, is to note some very tenuous and possibly suggestive connections without claiming in the least that they're deductive connections. In fact, they're not. They're at most vague and loose suggestions which perhaps are worth a little bit of thought" (p. 213). Although for Chomsky any move twoard a better society should be "predicated on some kind of assumption about human nature" (p. 214).

Panel 4: Chomsky, N., & Otero, C. *Language and Politics, expanded 2nd ed.* (Oakland, CA: AK Press, 2004), p. 468. The Bakunin quote is taken from Bakunin, M.A., & Lehning, A., *L'Empire knouto-germanique et la révolution sociale: 1870-1871* (Leiden: E.J. Brill, 1981).

Panels 5 and 6: Chomsky, N., & Otero, C. *Language and Politics, expanded 2nd ed.* (Oakland, CA: AK Press, 2004). Chomsky, N., "Language and Freedom" in Pateman, B. (ed.), *Chomsky on Anarchism* (Oakland, CA: AK Press, 2005), p. 113.

PAGE 18

Panel 2: Chomsky, N., & Otero, C. *Language and Politics, expanded 2nd ed.* (Oakland, CA: AK Press, 2004), p. 113.

PAGE 22

Panel 2: H.B. 2281 http://www.azleg.gov/legtext/49leg/2r/bills/hb2281s.pdf

PAGE 42

Panel 1: Chomsky, N., *Necessary Illusions: Thought Control in Democratic Societies* (Toronto: House of Anansi Press, 2003), p. 11.

Panel 2: Crozier, M. & Huntington, S., *The Crisis of Democracy: Report on the Governability of Democracies to the Trilateral Commission* (New York: New York University Press, 1975), p. 173.

PAGE 43

Panel 1-4: Chomsky, N., & Otero, C. *Language and Politics, expanded 2nd ed.* (Oakland, CA: AK Press, 2004), p. 264.

PAGE 44

Panel 1-5: Chomsky, N., Profit Over People: Neoliberalism and Global Order (New York: Seven Stories Press, 1999), pp. 47-48.

PAGE 48

Panel 3-5: Free Speech Movement: Mario Savio's speech before the FSM sit-in, December 3, 1964, Berkeley, CA. (n.d.) Retrieved January 20, 2014, from http://www.fsm-a.org/stacks/mario/mario_speech.htm.

PAGE 49-51

Cohen, R., *The Free Speech Movement: Reflections on Berkeley in the 1960s* (Berkeley, CA: University of California Press, 2002), pp. 64-65.

PAGE 88

Taylor, A., *Occupy!: Scenes from Occupied America* (London: Verso, 2011), pp. 52-53.

PAGE 91

Panel 5: Rau, A.B., "Arizona Tops Nation in College Cuts, Tuition Hikes," *The Arizona Republic,* May 13, 2015.

ACKNOWLEDGMENTS

Thanks to Noam Chomsky for taking the time to sit down and talk to me. Countless lessons of what solidarity means can be learned from that simple act.

Thanks to Anthony Arnove and Jessie Kindig for their counsel, guidance, and importantly, believing in this project.

Thanks to Dan Simon for his editing work. I'm looking forward to learning more writing tips you gleaned from your time with Zinn and Studs. Many thanks to all at Seven Stories Press.

I'm grateful to Jay Jacot for going above and beyond lettering work. Who would've thought two kids from Mason, Michigan, would be making comic books.

Thanks to Max Lieberman and Bryan O'Neal for the crowdfunding video work.

Many thanks to Guille Mason for his counsel on crowdfunding and much more. *Visca Barca!*

Thanks to Adam Szlachetka, Mike Litos, and Dan Domanowski for reading over numerous drafts of this book.

I'm indebted to the 107 crowdfunding supporters who believed in this project. Thank you for your patience as this book took much longer to come into the world than I anticipated.

Saige, Tess, and Norah—the future truly inspires me.

Thanks to Mom and Dad. The foundation you helped create made this book possible.

And to Rachel—my first editor, collaborator, and best friend—"thank you" seems too small a phrase, so I'll just say this: You are a living example of how to be gentle and kind.